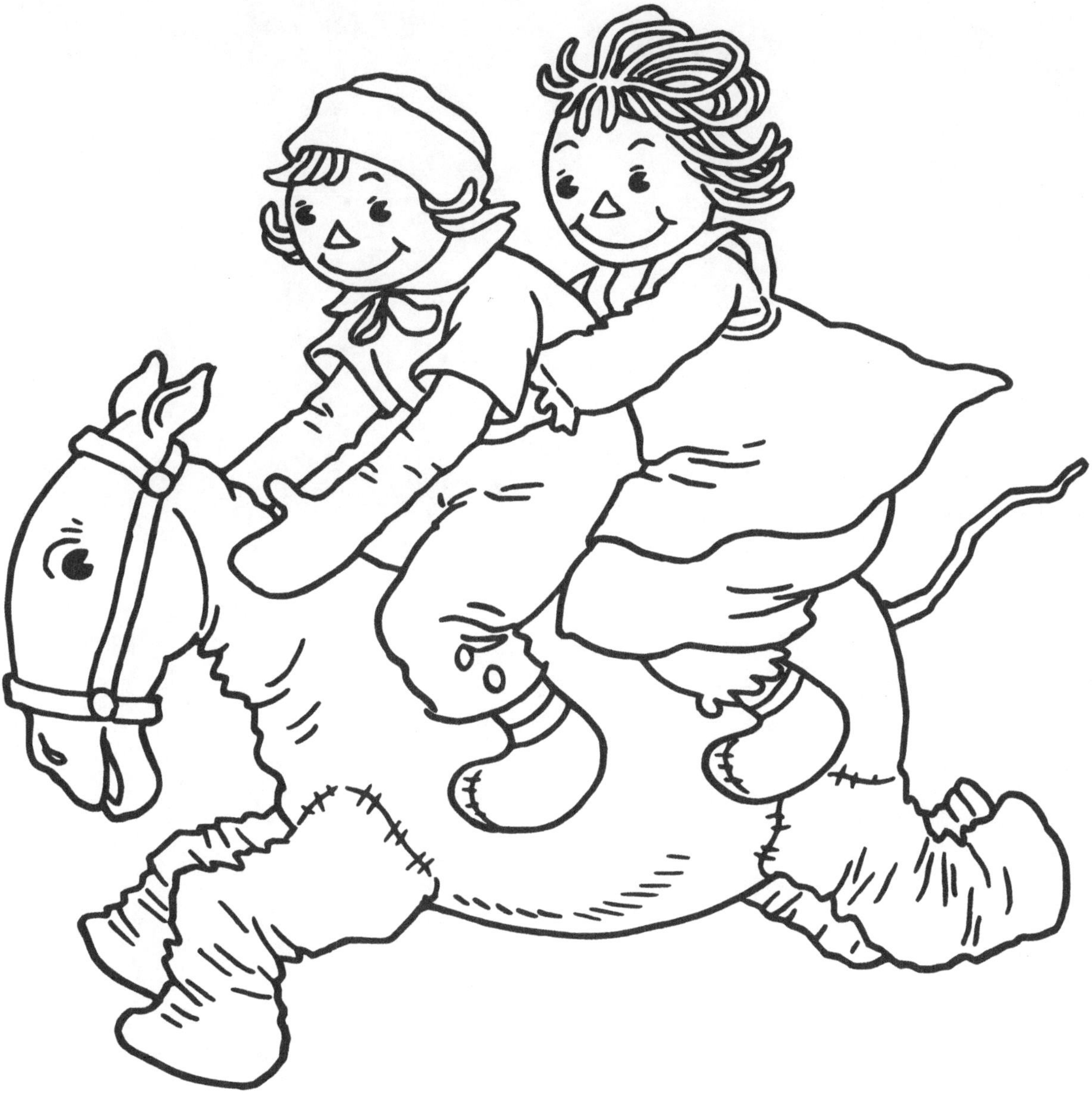

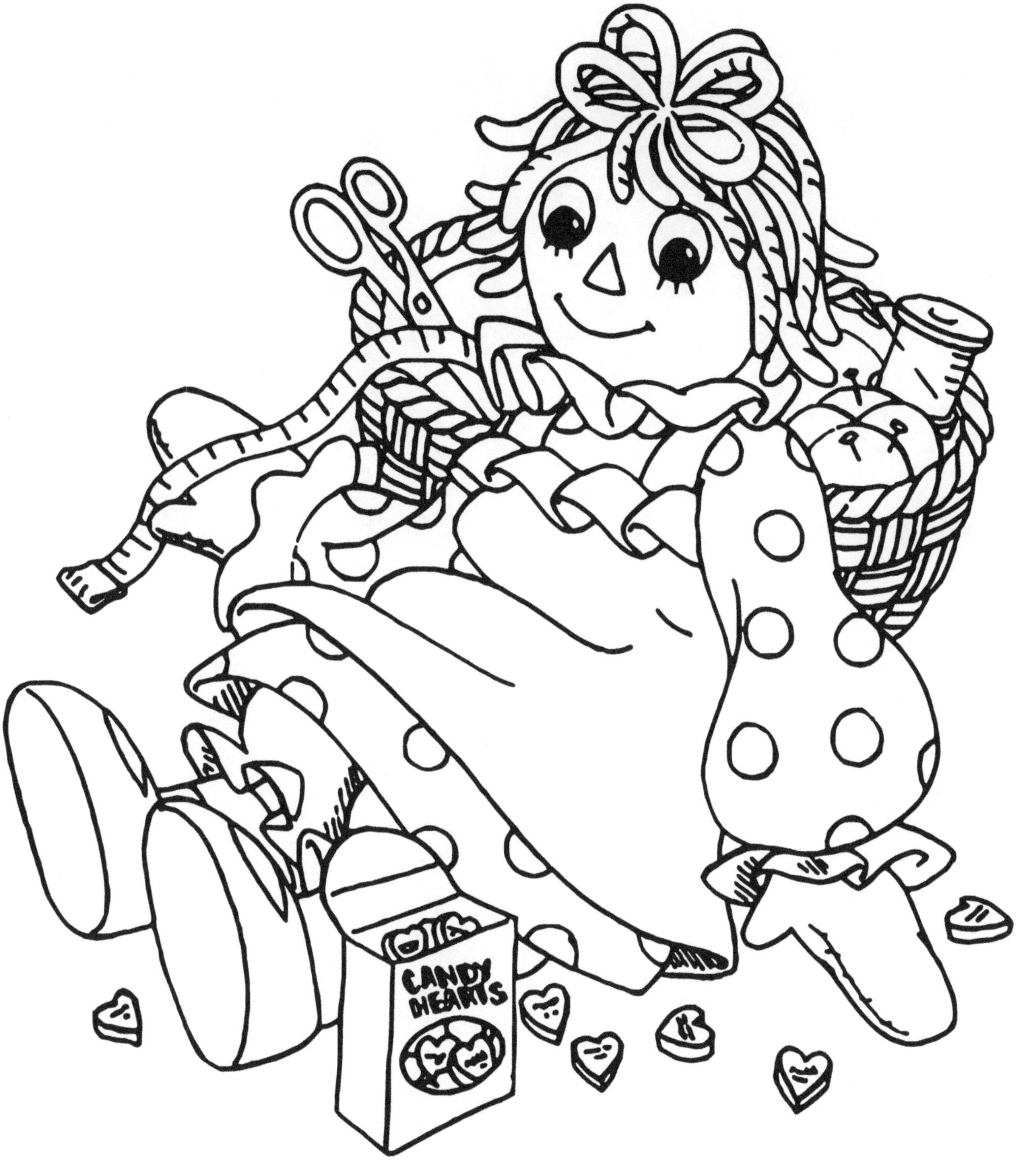
CANDY
HEARTS

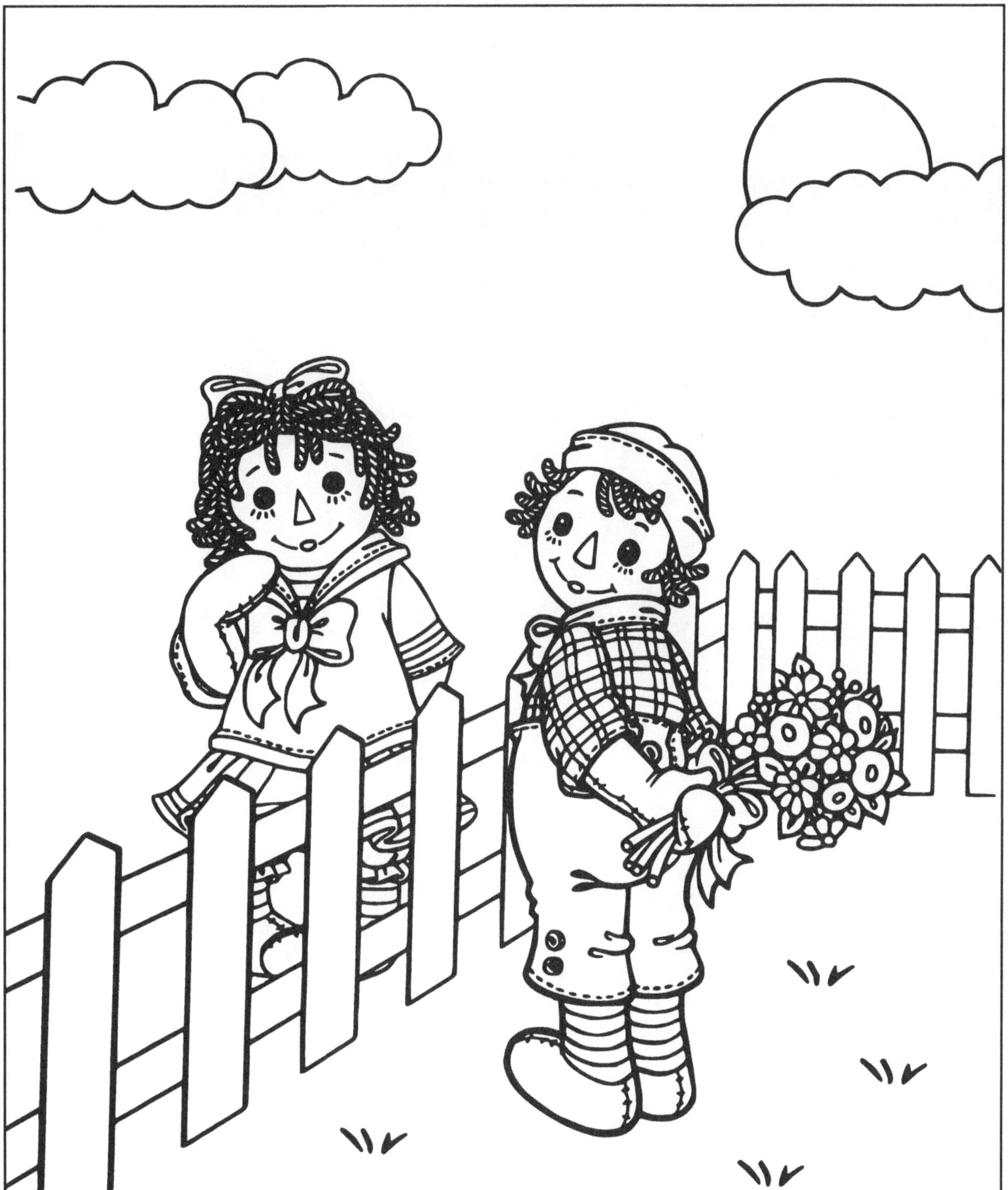

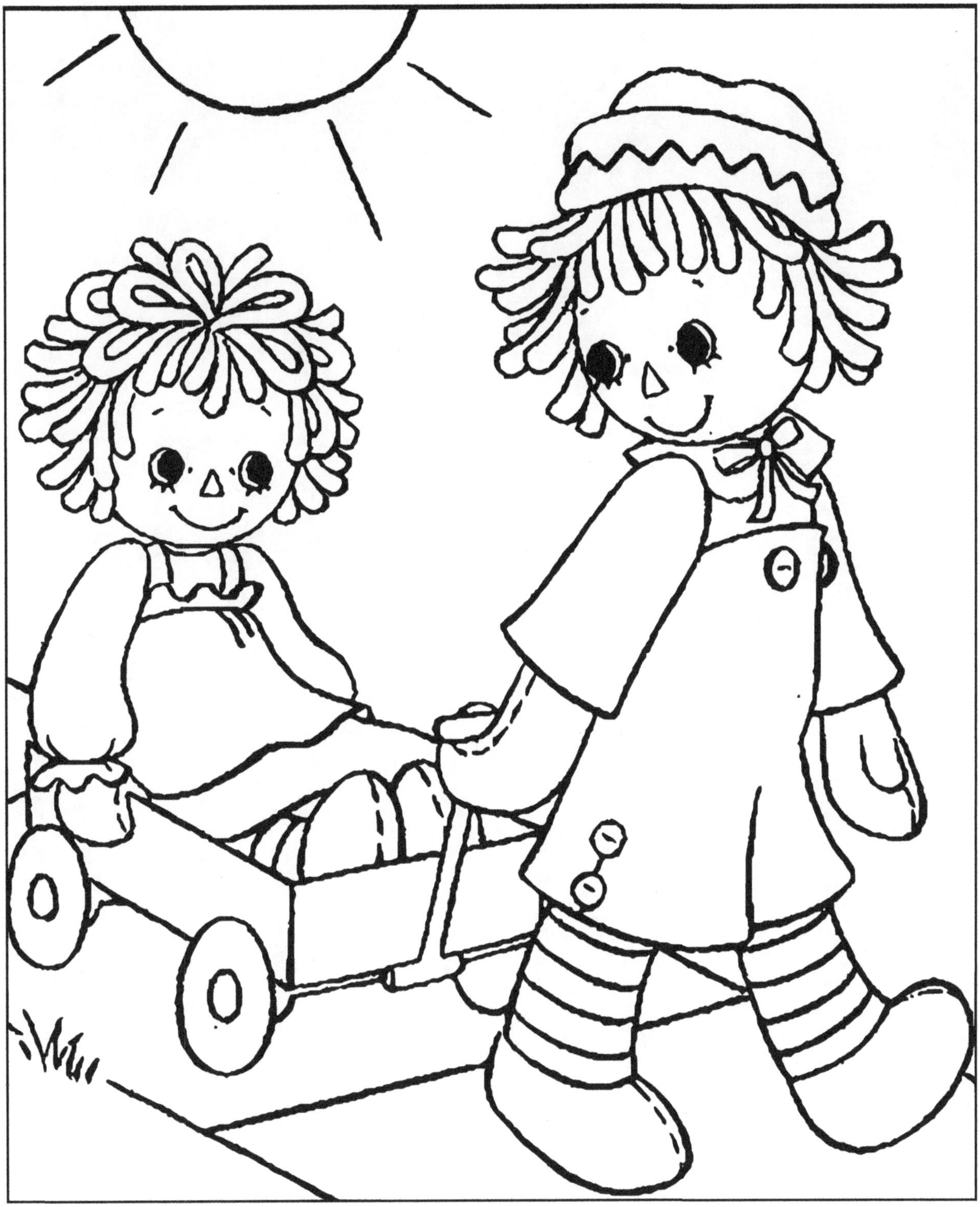

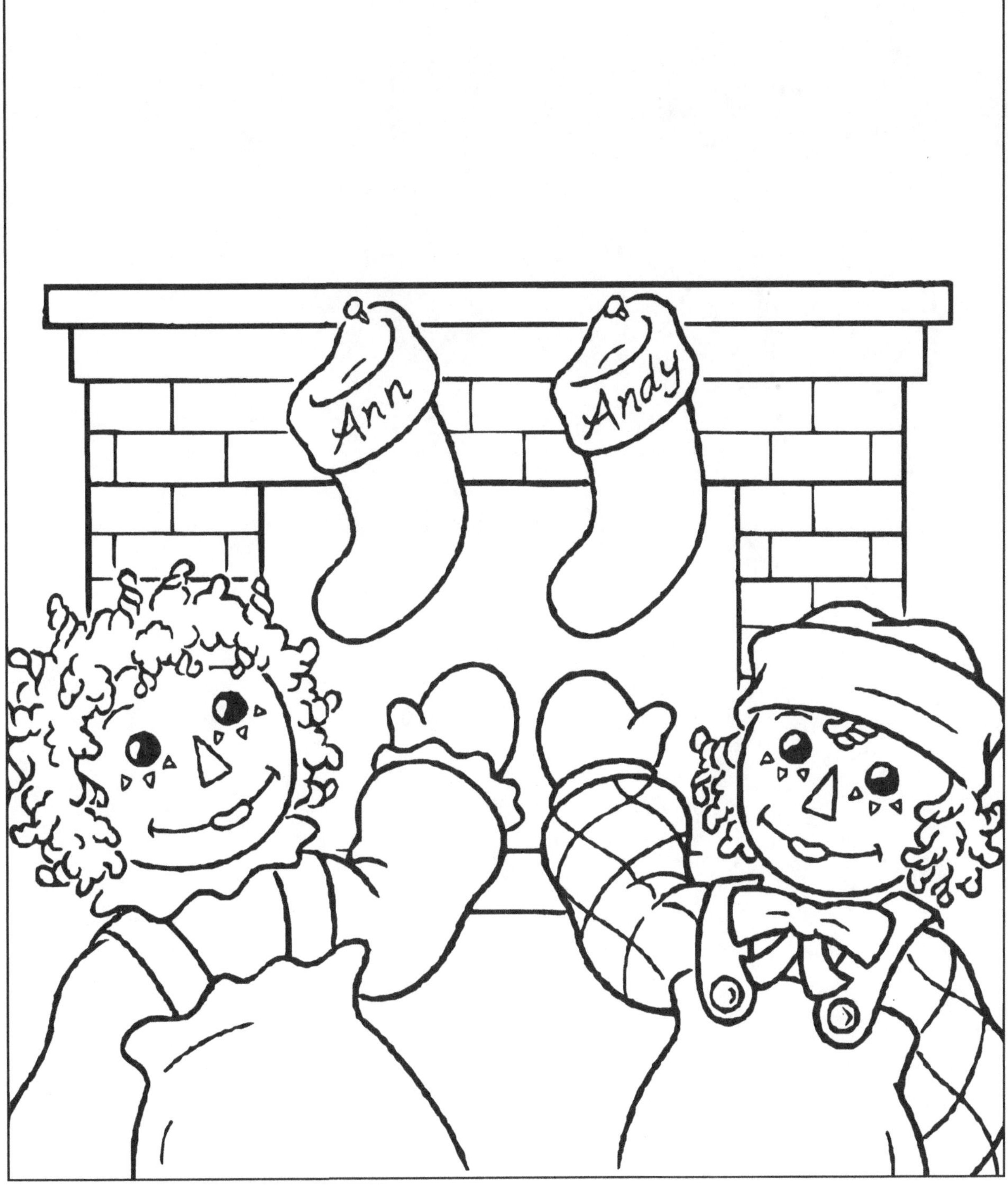
Ann
Andy

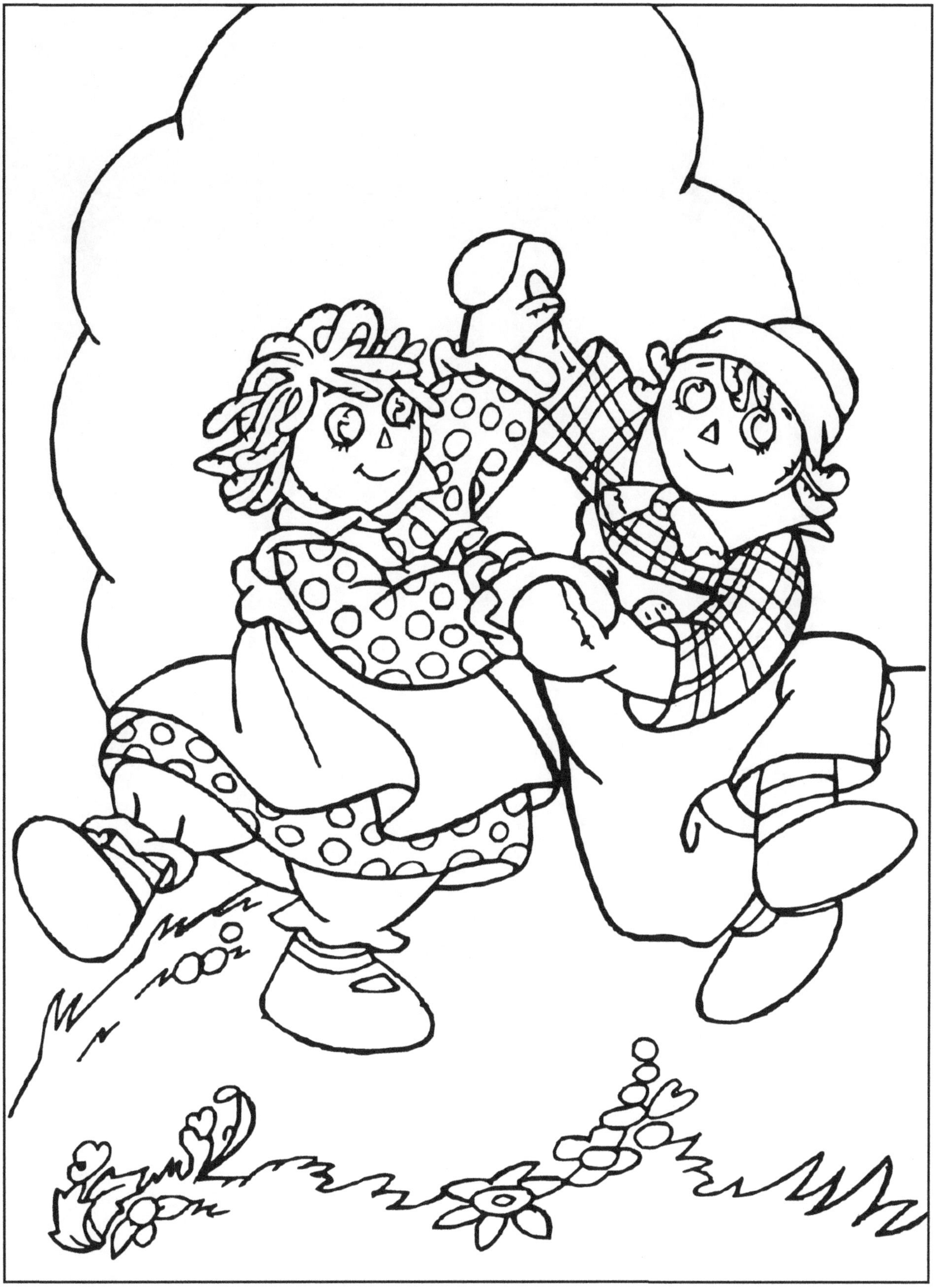

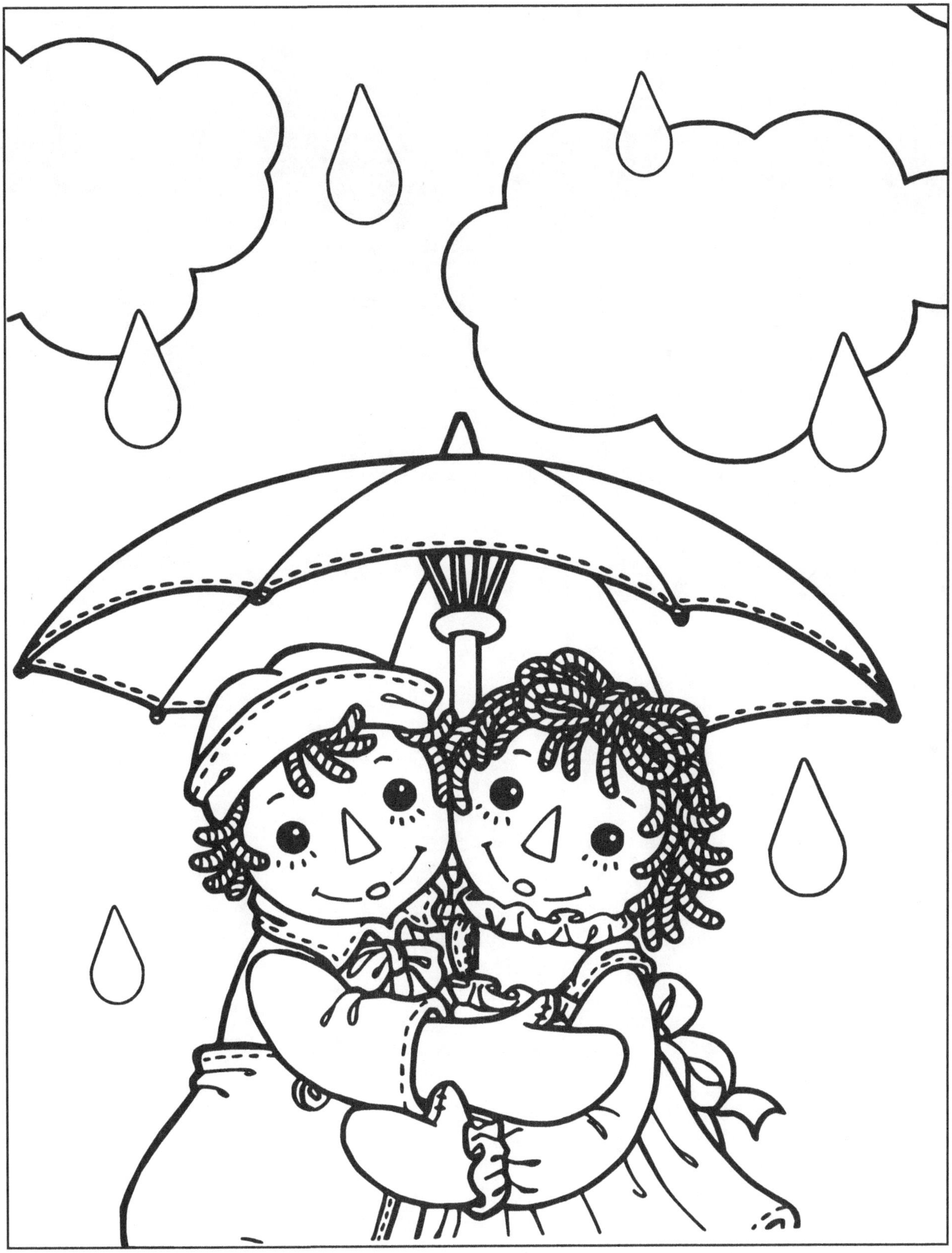

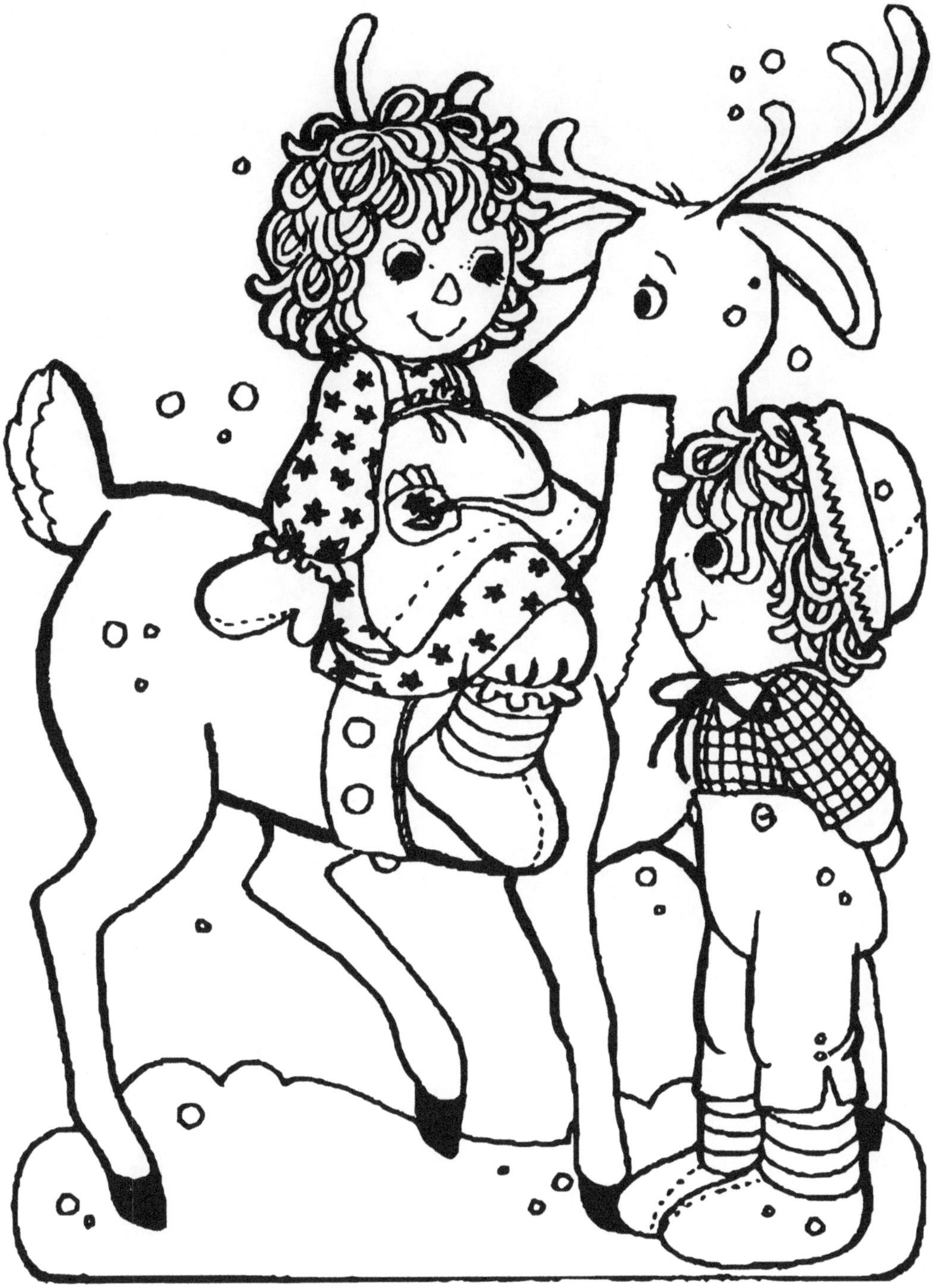

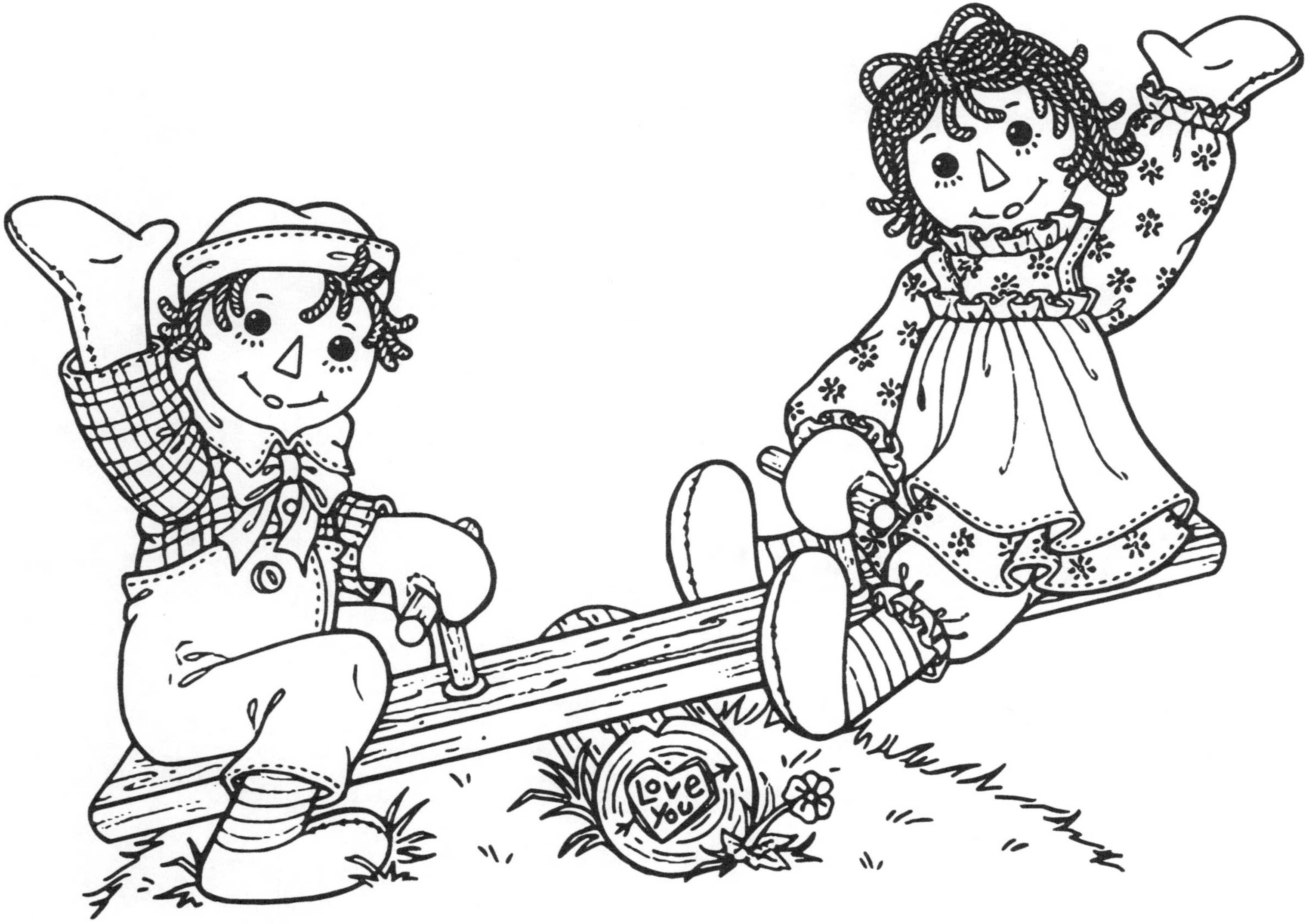
Love You

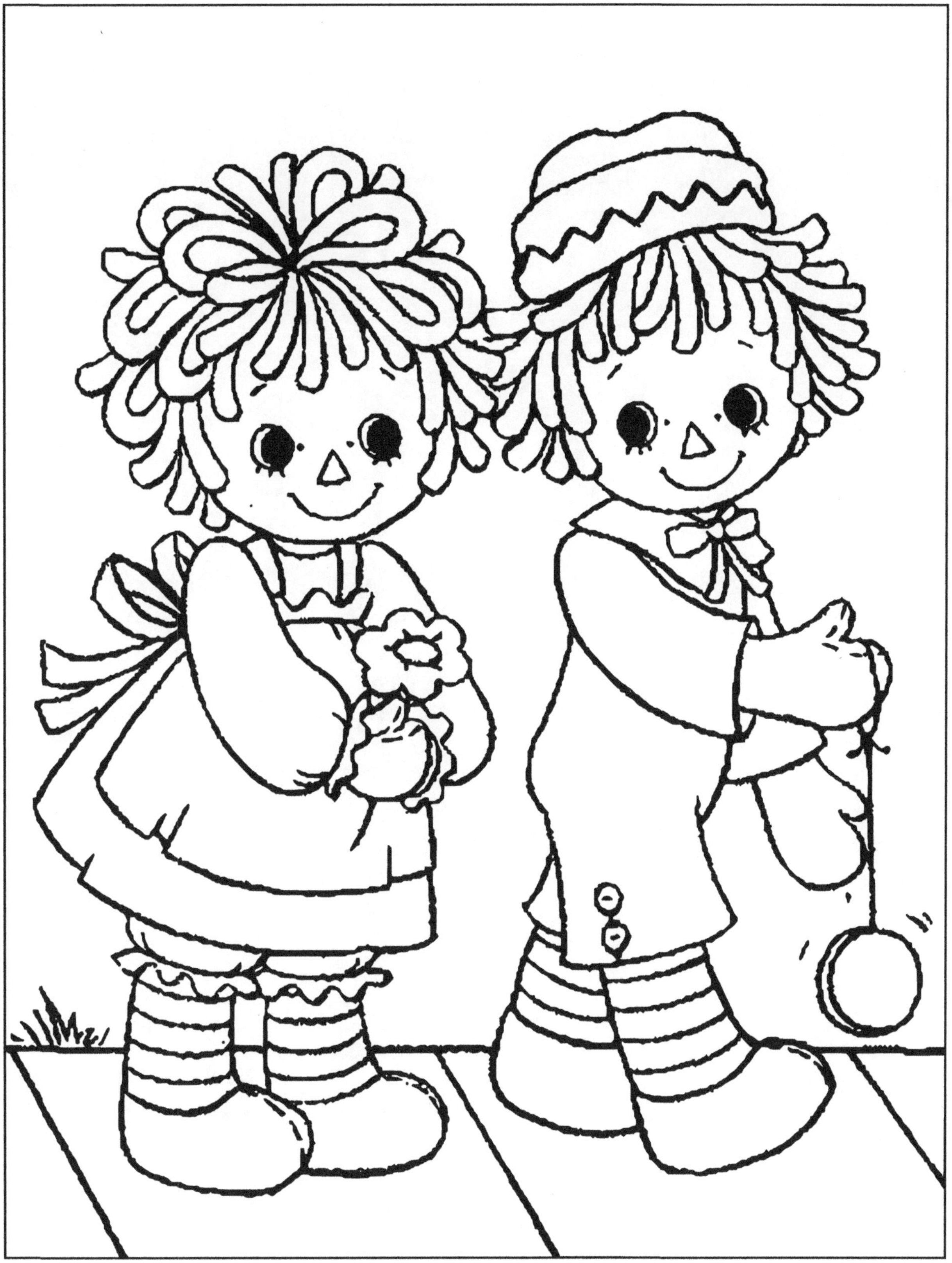

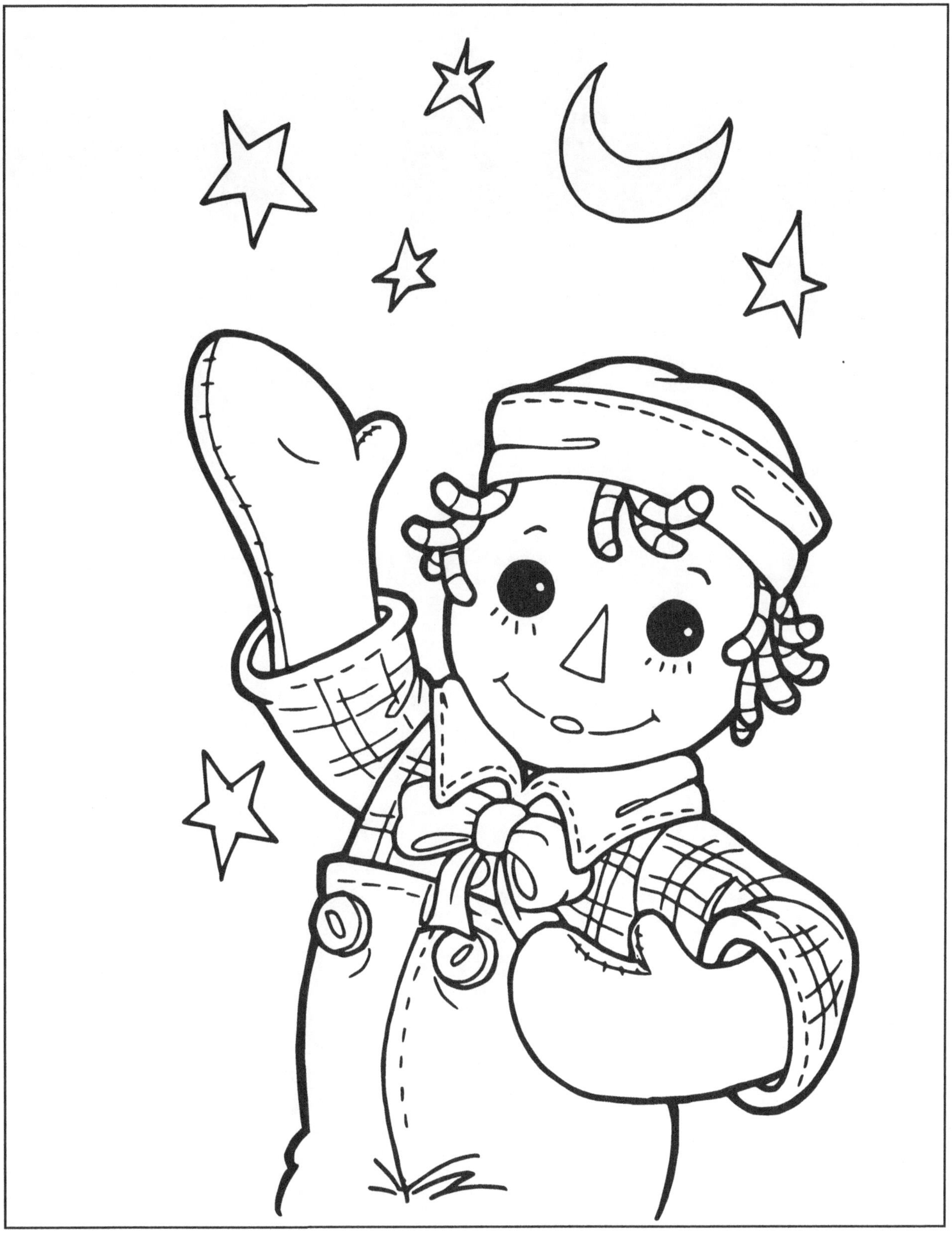

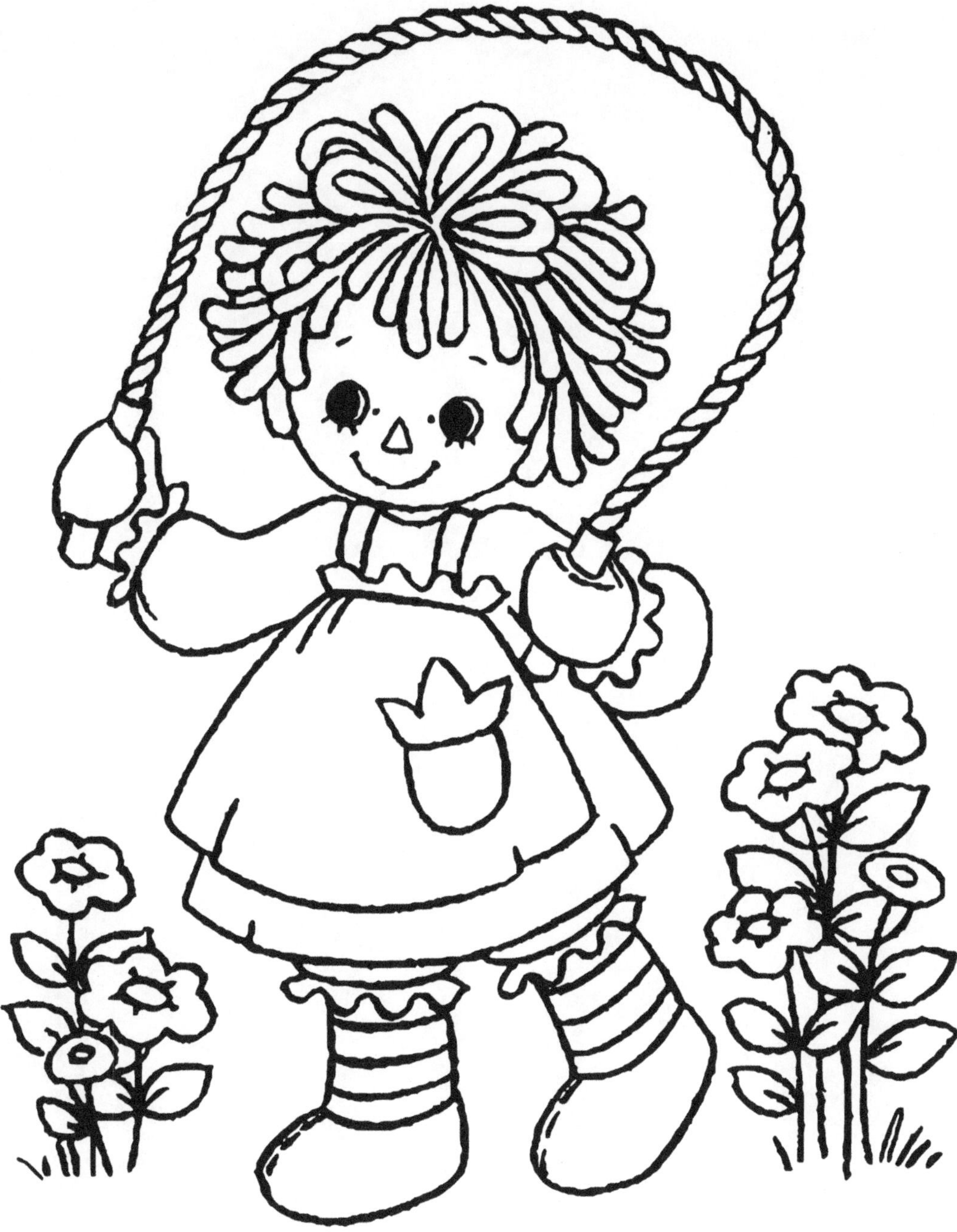

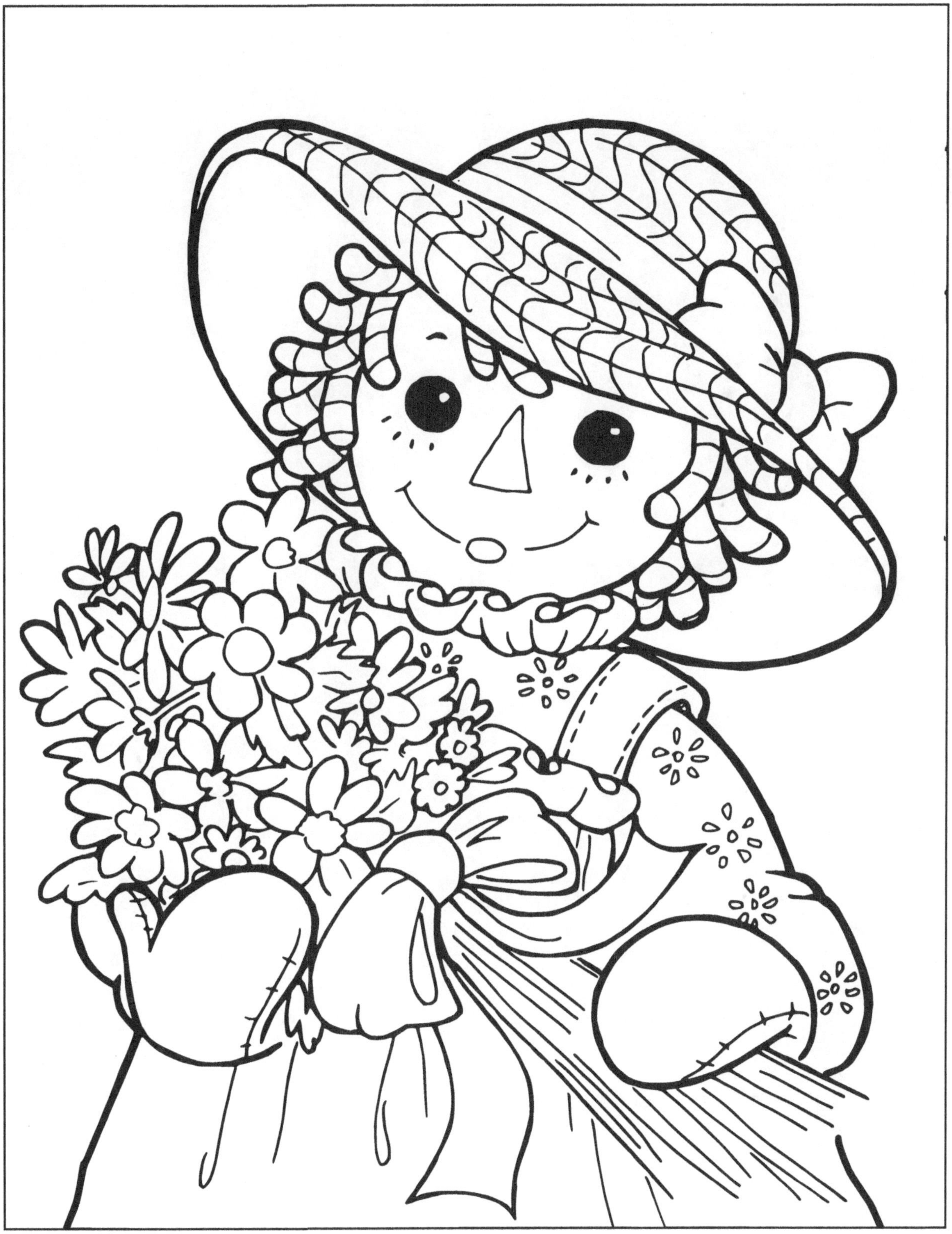

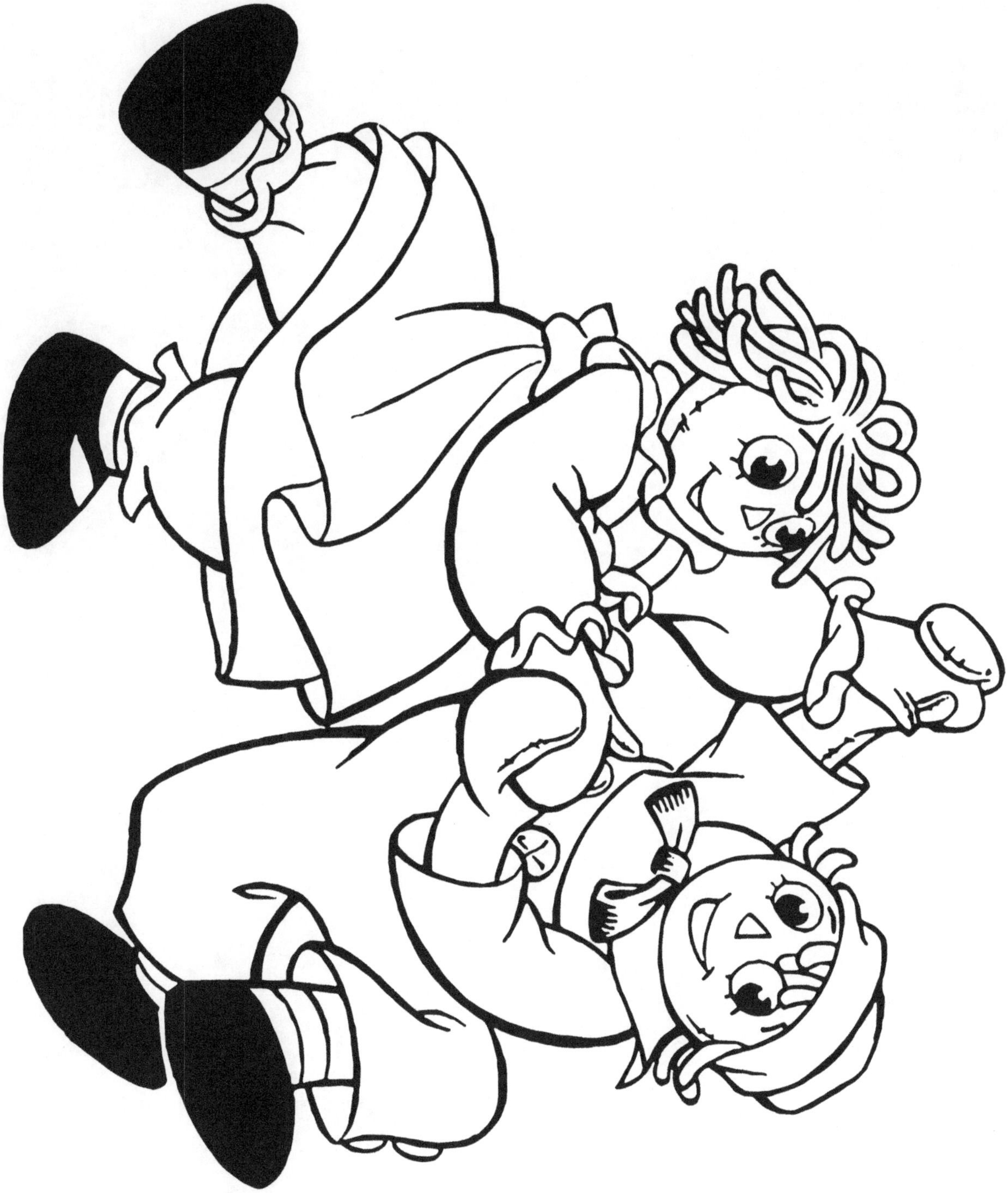

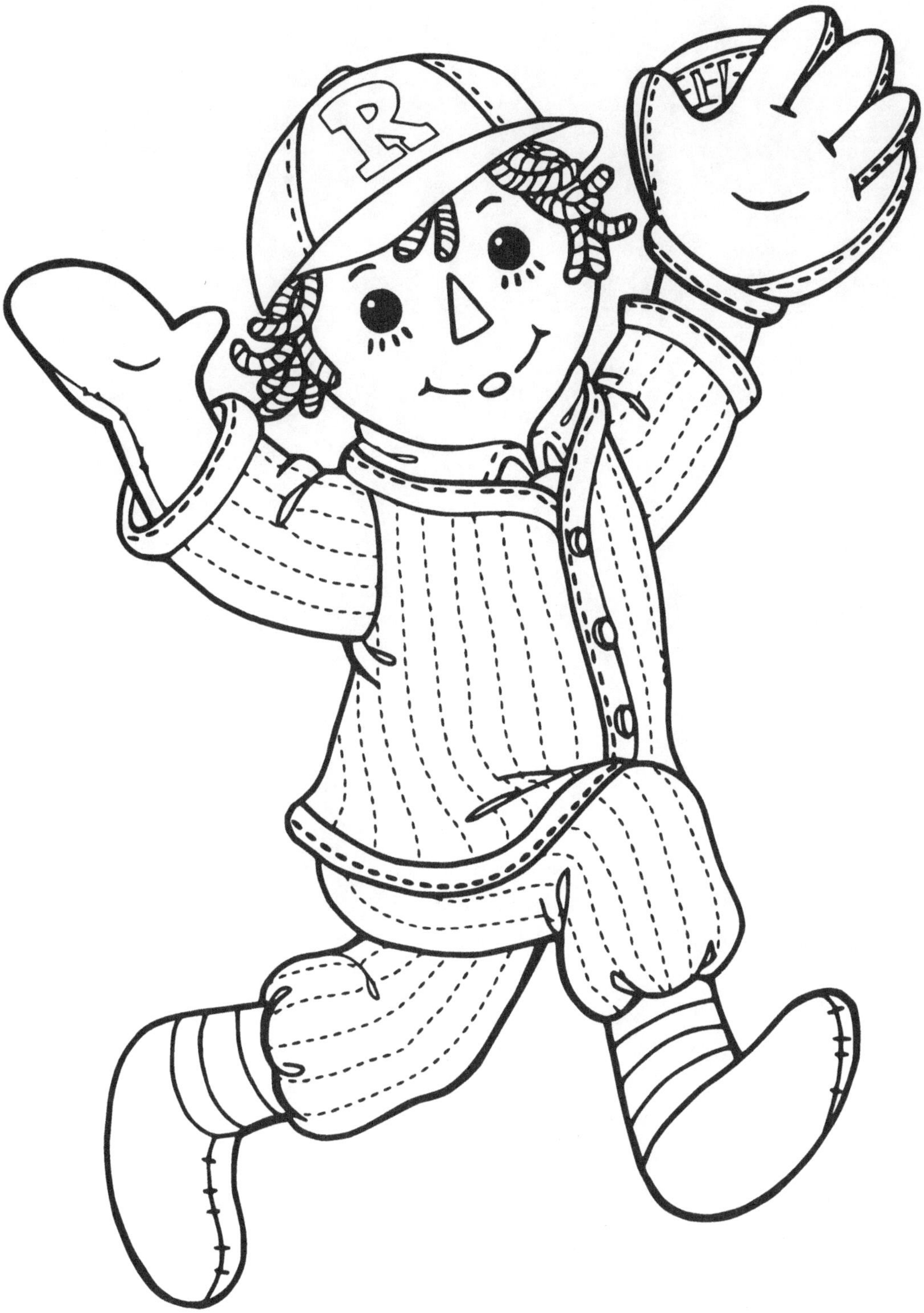
R

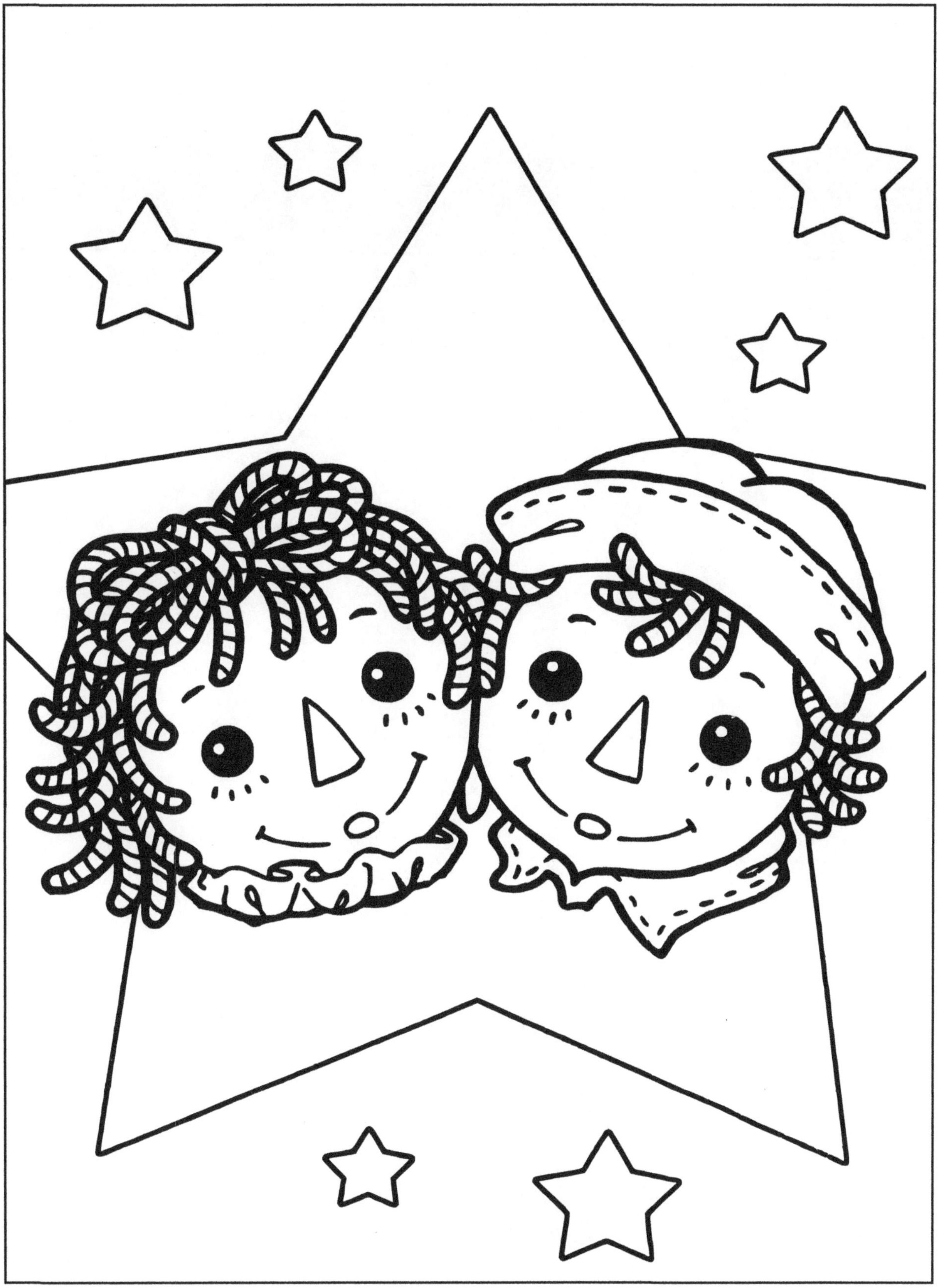

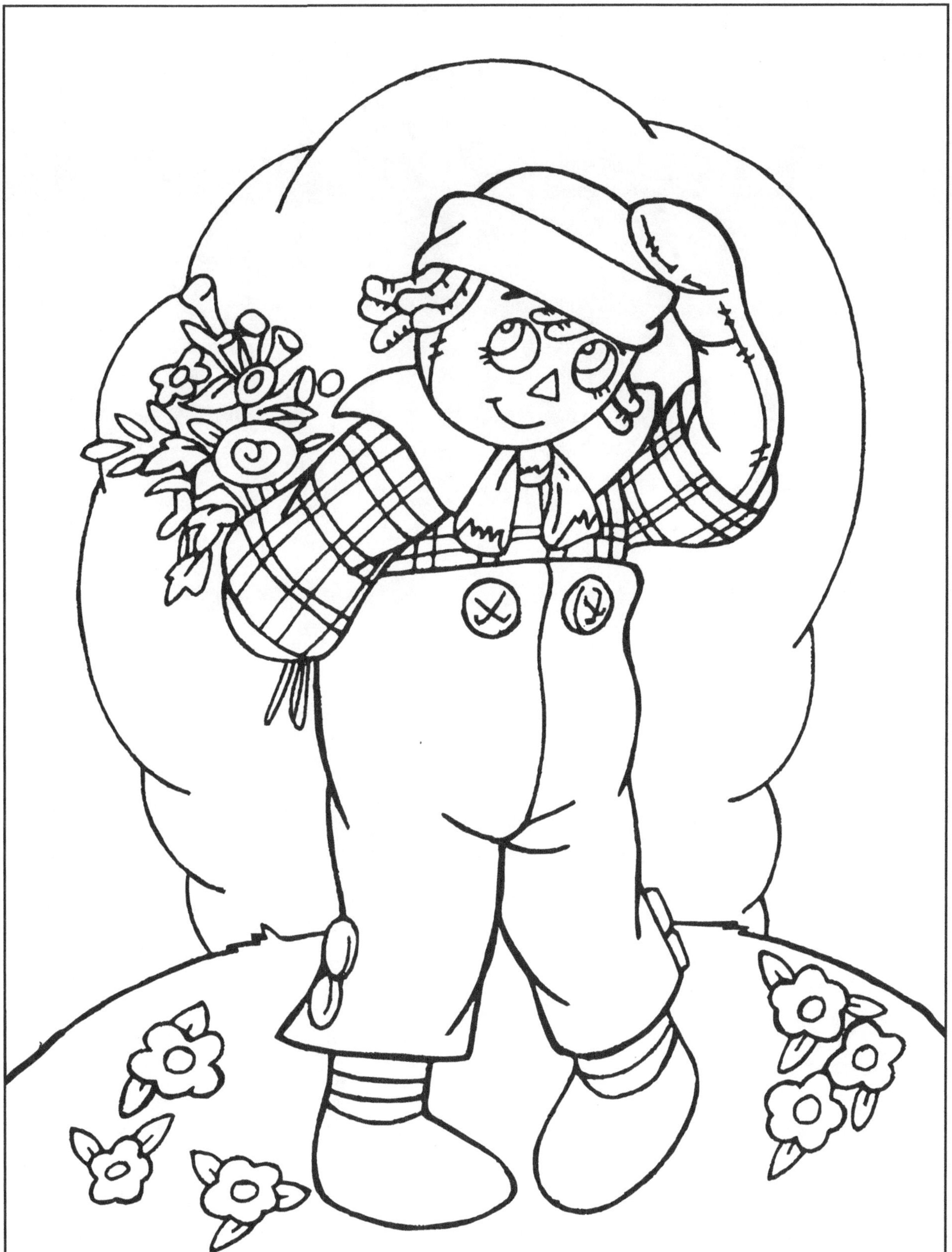

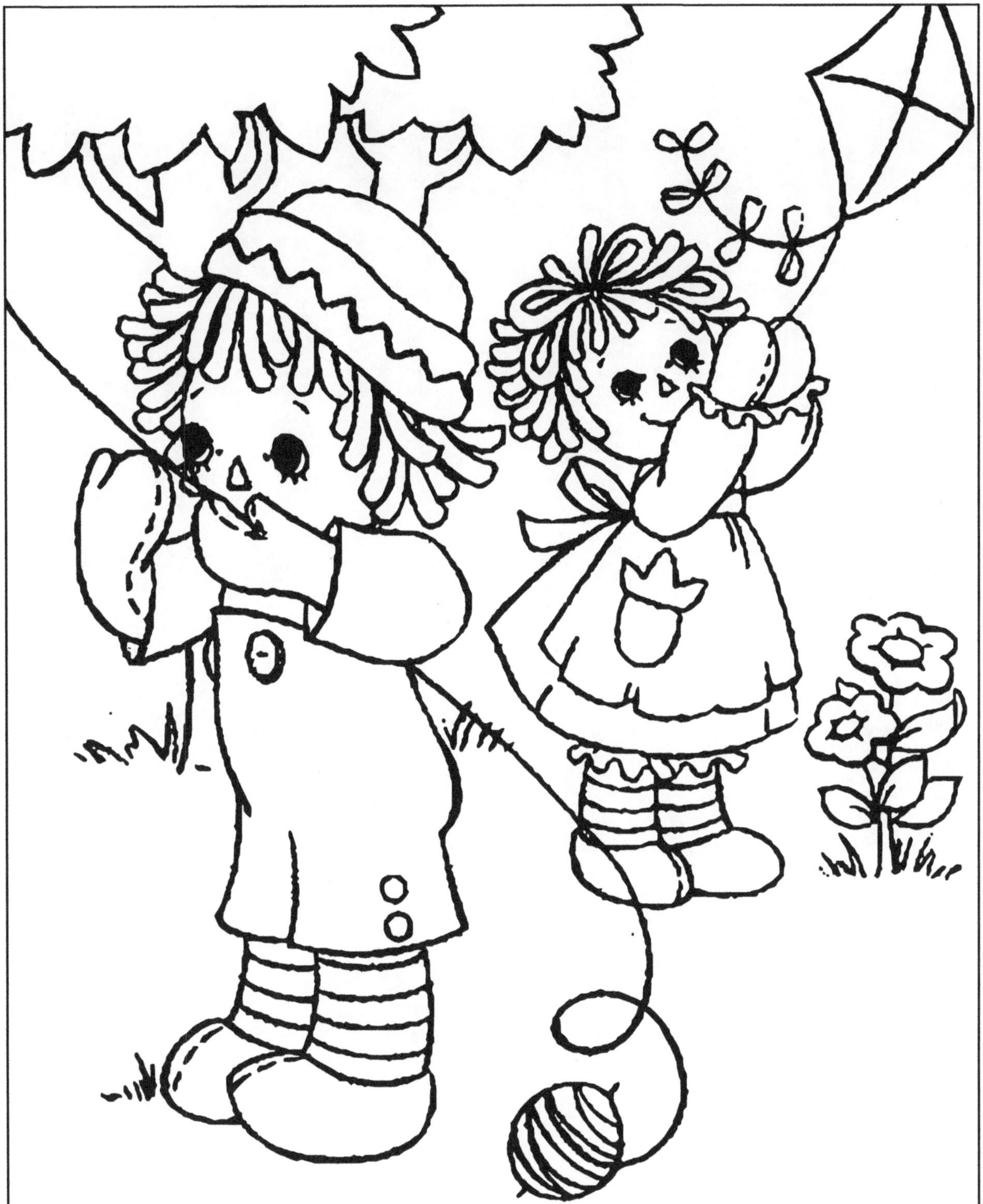

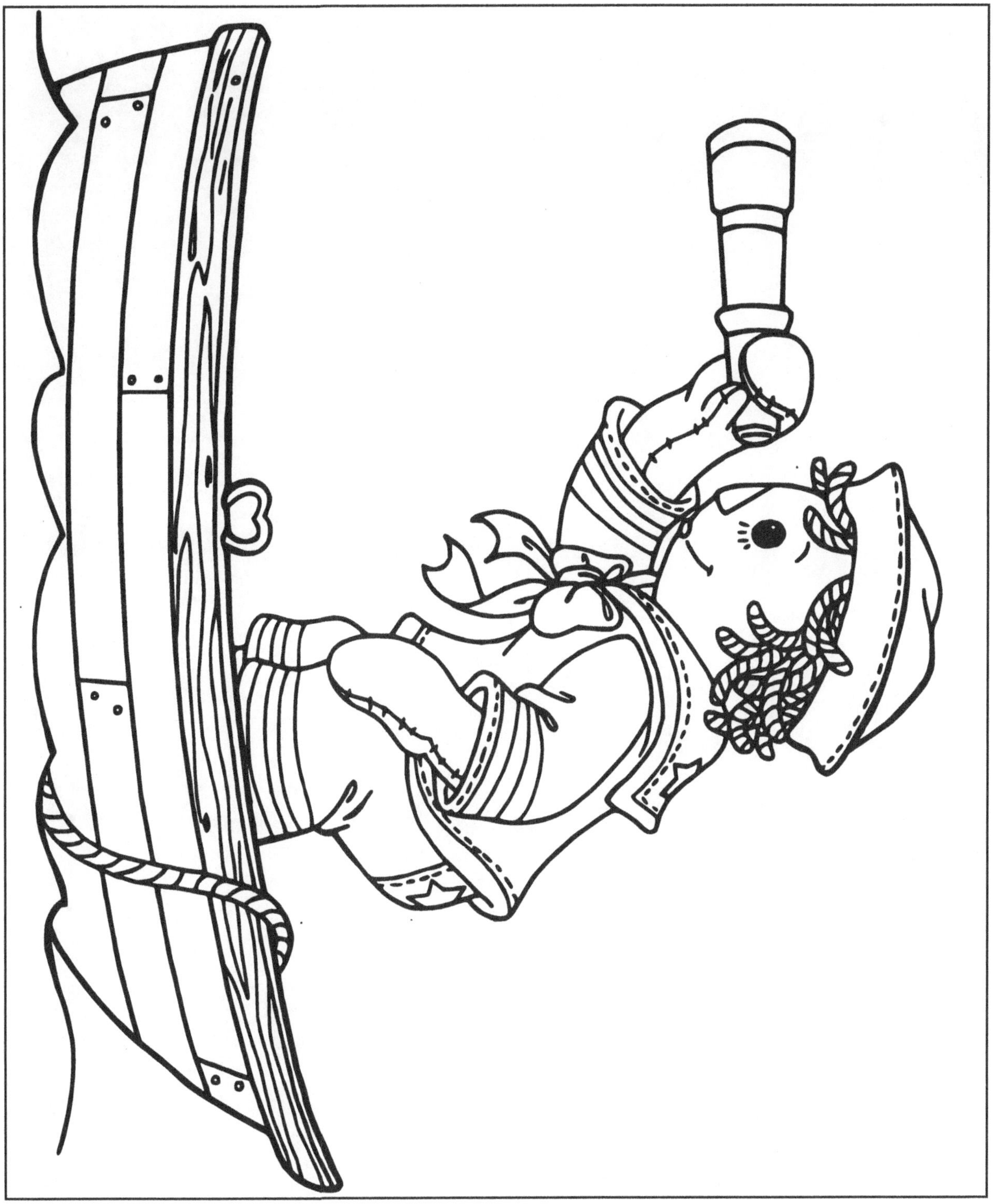

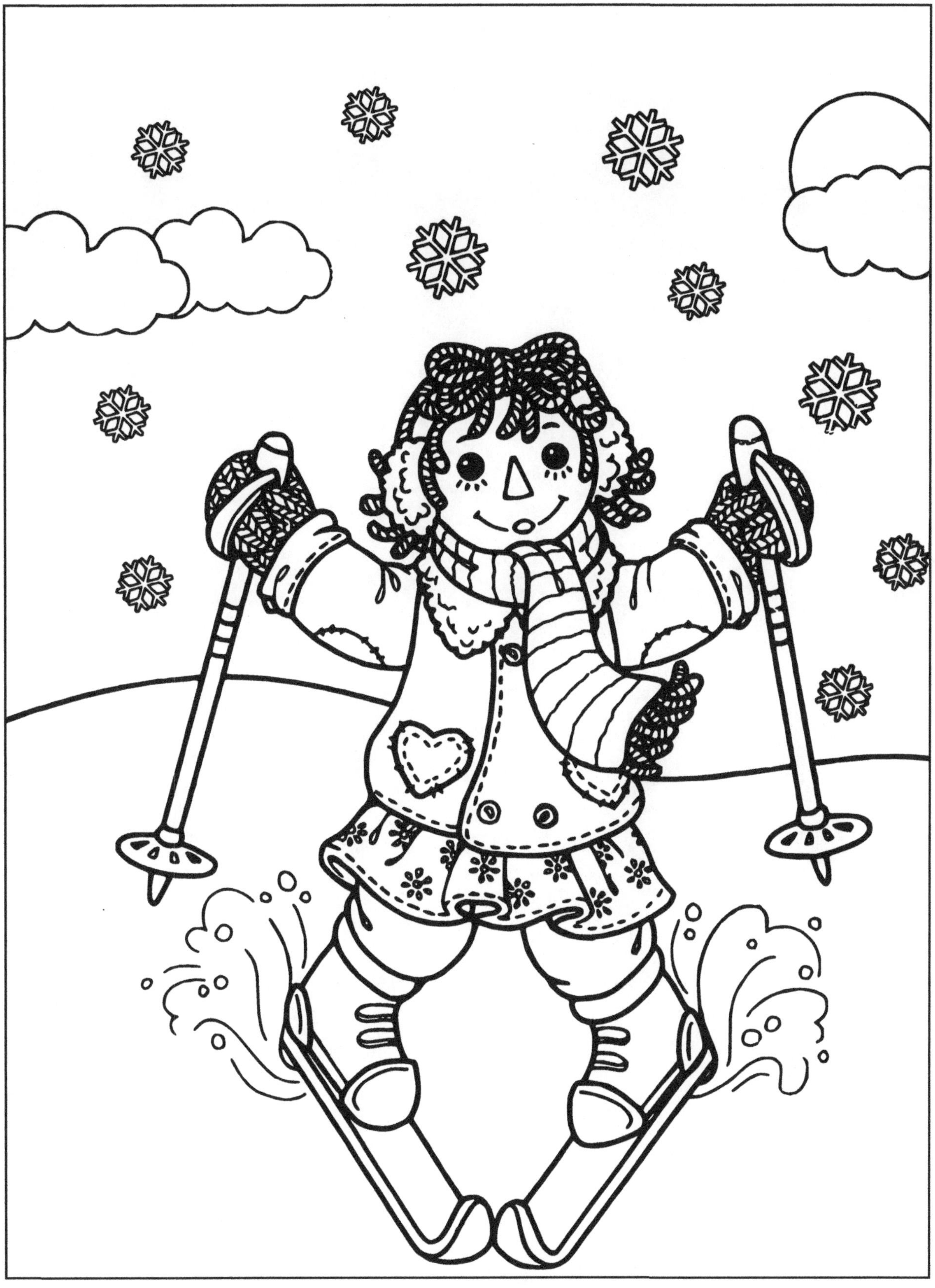

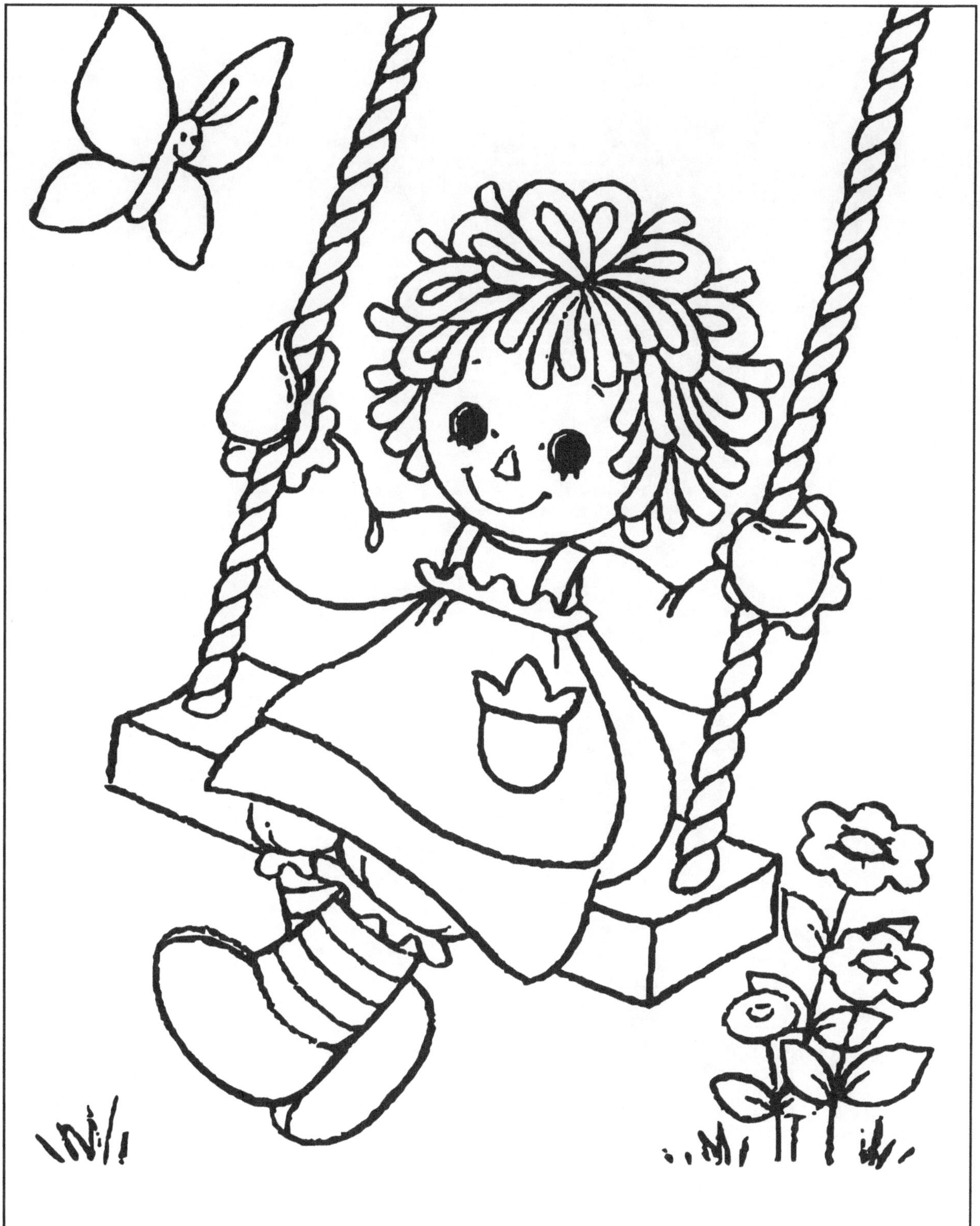

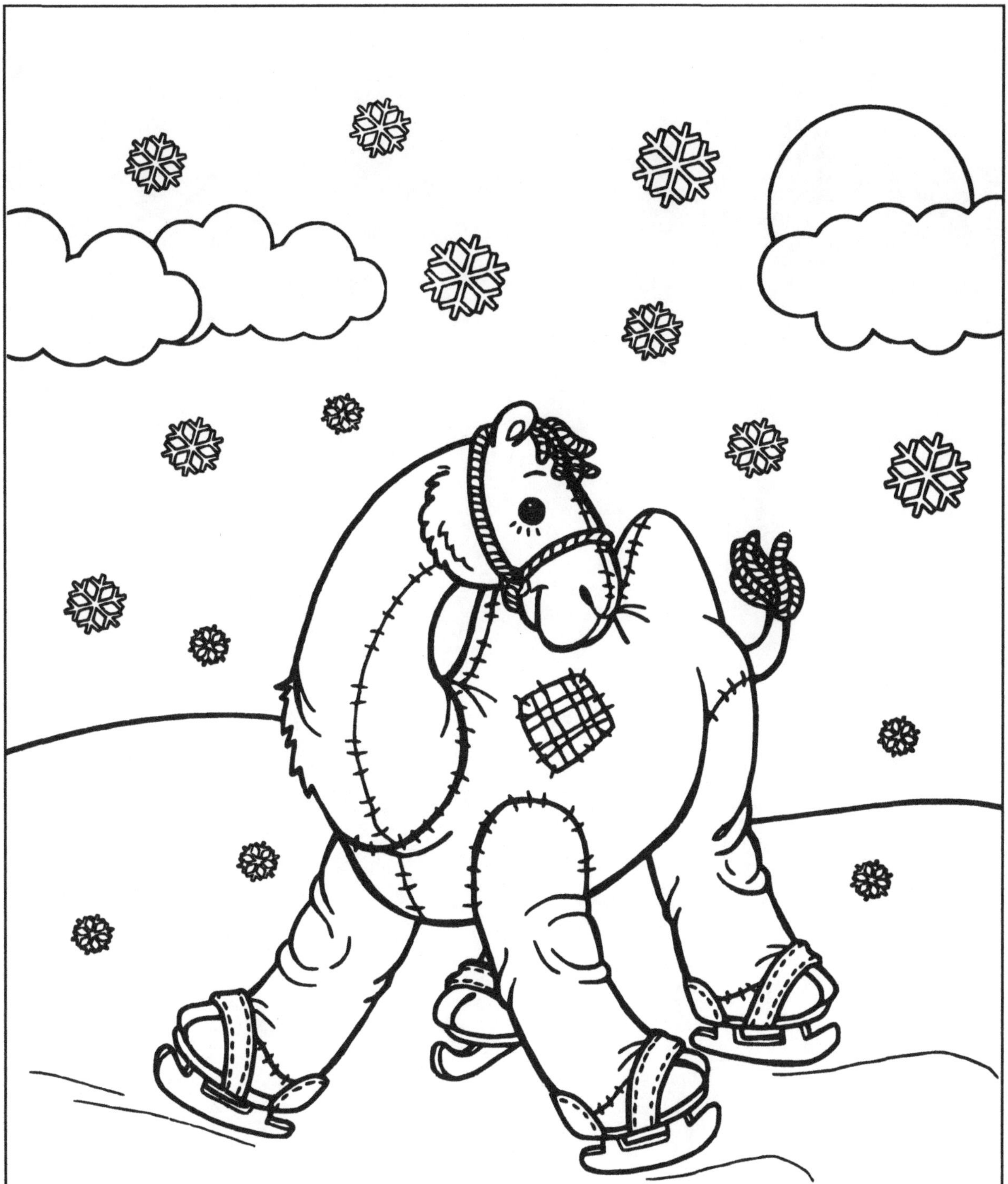

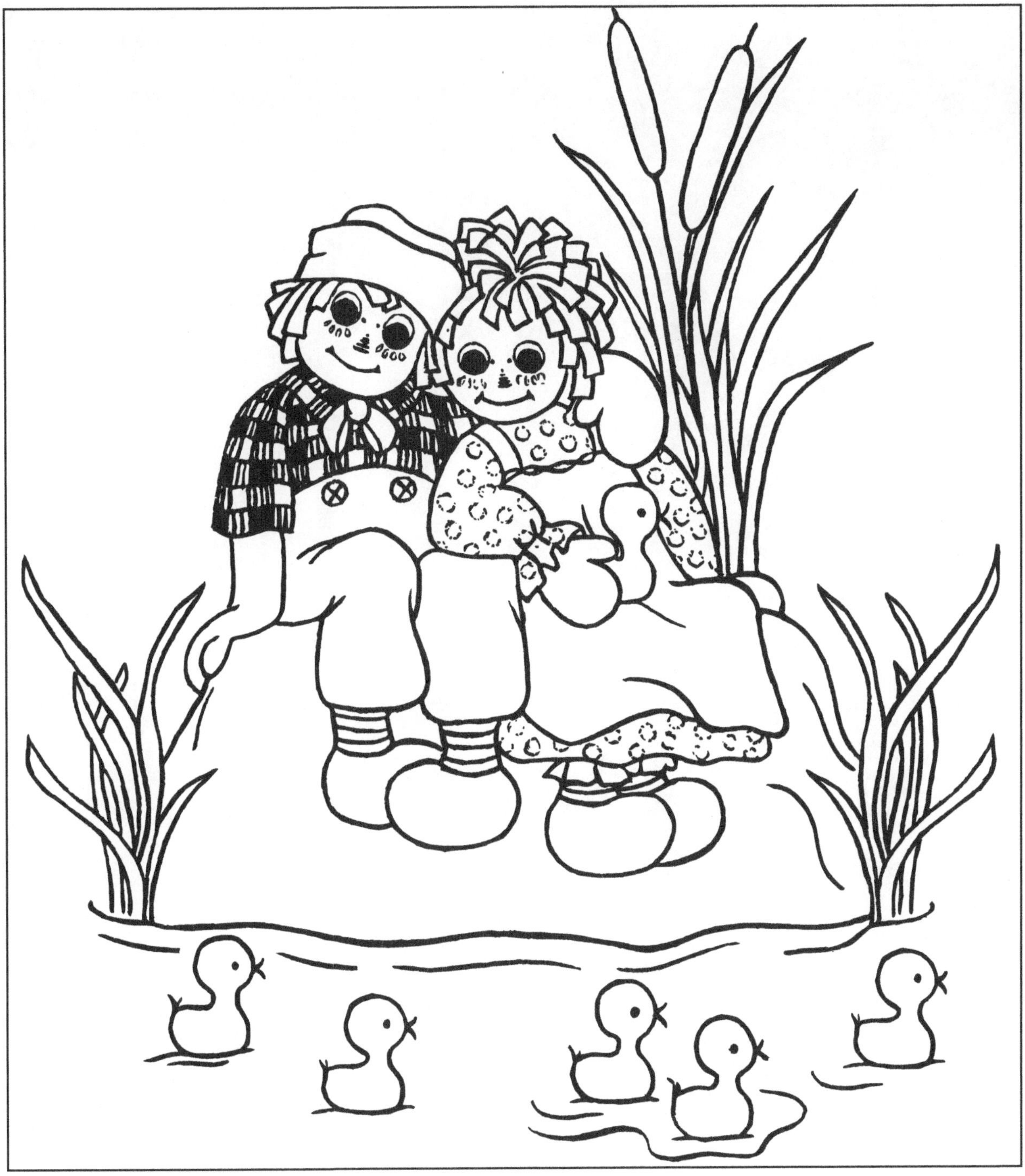

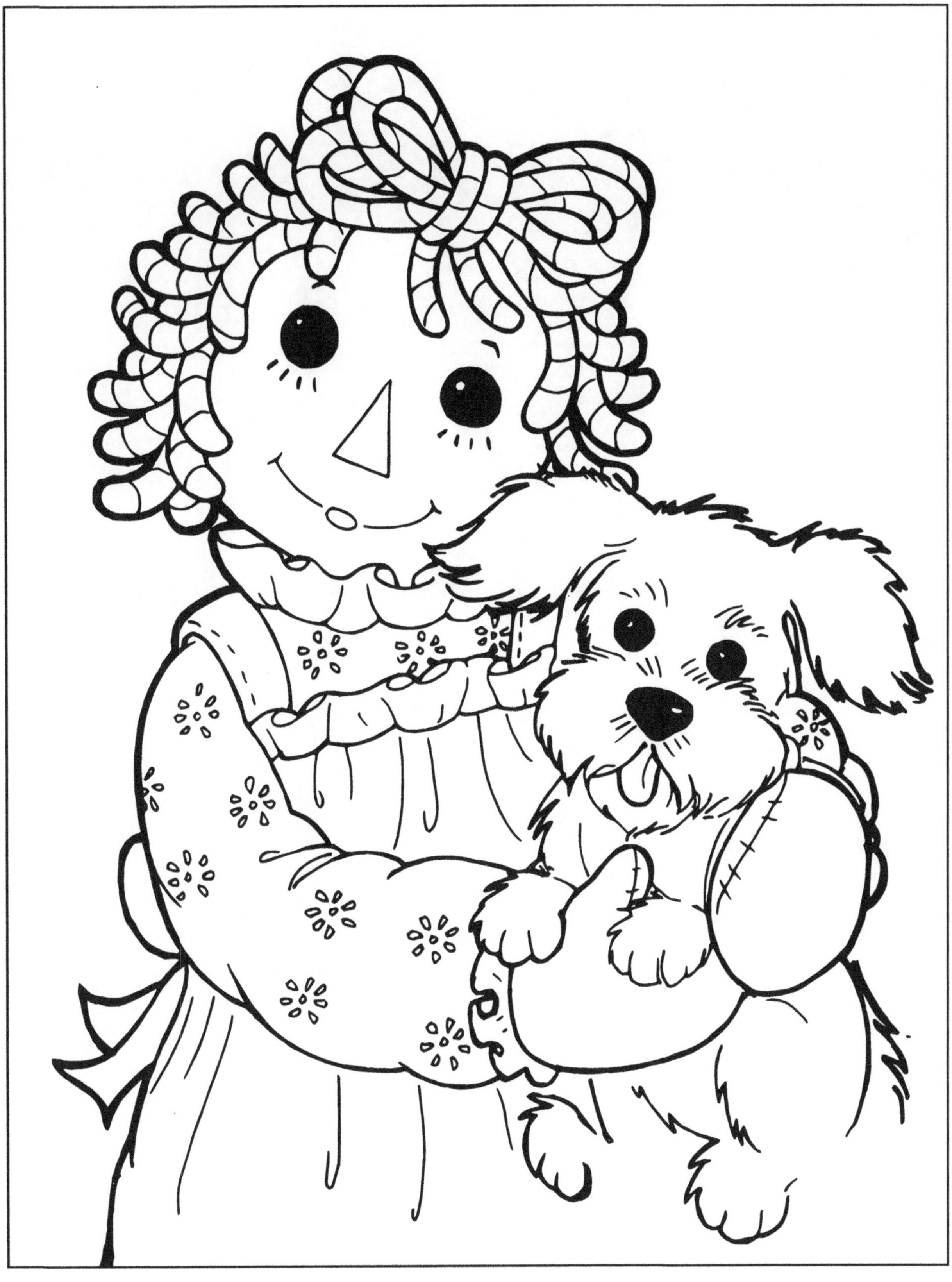

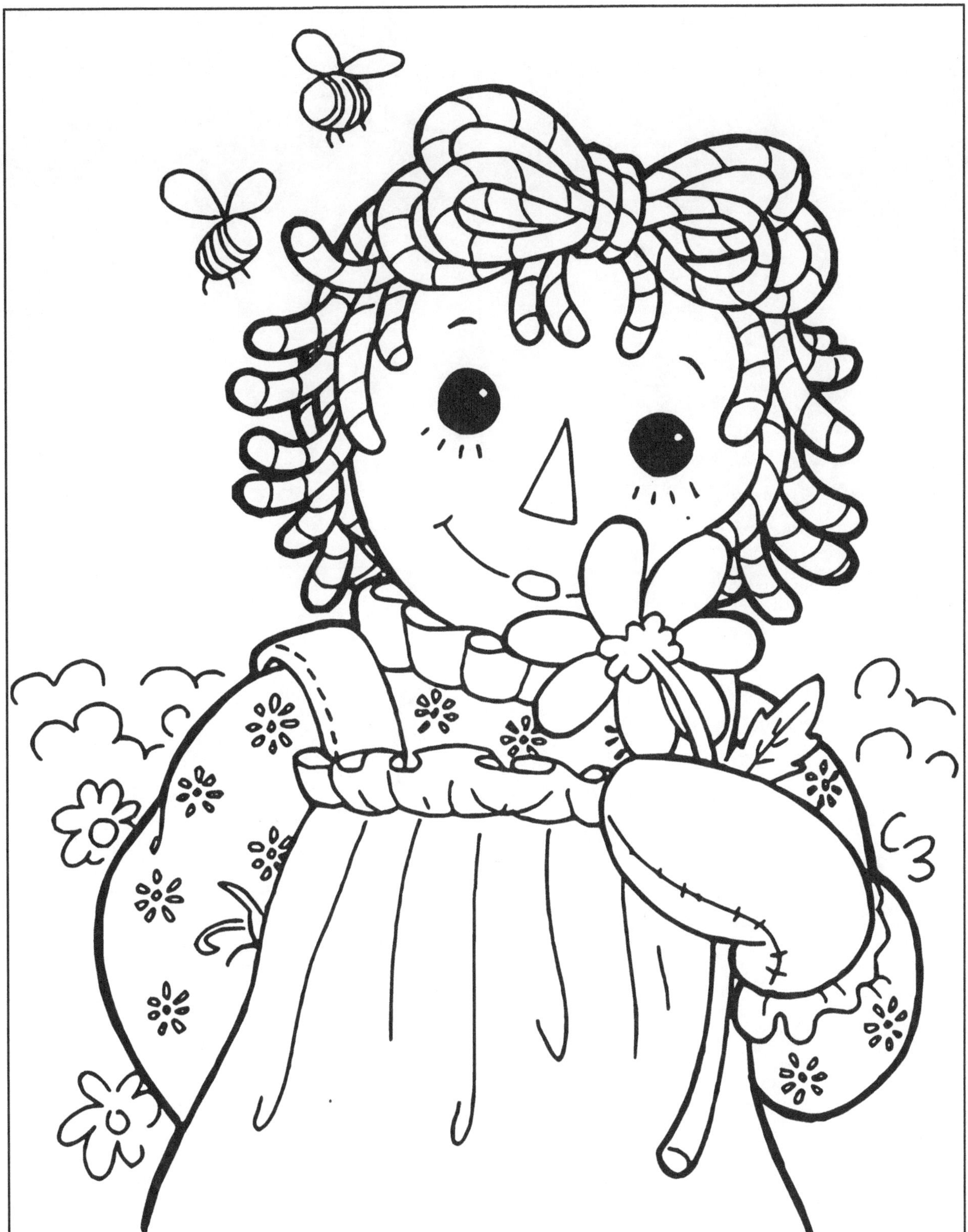

Made in the USA
Las Vegas, NV
10 October 2024

96618835R00031